RUNNING LIGHTS

RUNNING LIGHTS

POEMS BY

HENRY CARLILE

Dragon Gate, Inc.
PORT TOWNSEND, WASHINGTON

LC #80-067971

ISBN 0-937872-00-8 (cloth)
0-937872-01-6 (paper)

First Printing, 1981

Published by Dragon Gate, Inc., 508 Lincoln Street,
Port Townsend, Washington 98368.

ACKNOWLEDGMENTS

Grateful acknowledgment is made to the following publications in which these poems first appeared:

The American Poetry Review: Flying

Antaeus: The Burned Girl; Flood Control; Giant Ocean Sunfish; Listening to Beethoven on the Oregon Coast

Antioch Review: One Book; Running Lights; Stalking Morels

The Chowder Review: Grace

Concerning Poetry: Spider Reeves

The Iowa Review: Depression; The Dream of Execution; Havana Blues; The Four Seasons

Ironwood: Surgery

The Malahat Review: The Camera

The Missouri Review: The New City

The New Yorker: The Cardinal

The Ohio Review: In the More Recent Past

Oregon East: Clean Symmetrical Furrows

Poetry: Dodo (reprinted in *A Geography of Poets,* edited by Edward Field, Bantam Books, 1979)

Poetry Northwest: Butchering Crabs; "Go Study the Spots on a Daffodil"; Incomplete Description of "The World's Smallest Church Grotto"; My Father; Take the Bass for Example; The Book of the Deer, the Bear and the Elk; 0°

Poetry Now: The Barber's Fountain

The Portland Review: The Bird Man of Redmond; For a Friend Drowned Off Grays Harbor; Exposures

Prairie Schooner: Small Hunting Accident

Special thanks are due to the National Endowment for the Arts for their generous award of a grant which allowed me to complete many of these poems in 1977 and 1978.

—H.C.

CONTENTS

I

11 Flying
12 The Barber's Fountain
13 Grace
14 Depression
15 My Father
16 Havana Blues
17 The Camera
19 Exposures
21 The Book of the Deer, the Bear and the Elk

II

25 Running Lights
26 Butchering Crabs
28 Take the Bass for Example
29 For a Friend Drowned Off Grays Harbor
30 Giant Ocean Sunfish
31 Spider Reeves
33 Listening to Beethoven on the Oregon Coast

III

37 Incomplete Description of "The World's Smallest Church Grotto"
39 Clean Symmetrical Furrows
40 0°
41 Dodo
42 The Bird Man of Redmond
44 The Cardinal

45 Surgery
46 "Go Study the Spots on a Daffodil"
47 Stalking Morels
48 Flood Control

IV

53 In the More Recent Past
54 The Burned Girl
55 The Dream of Execution
56 Small Hunting Accident
58 One Book
59 The Four Seasons
"In the shape of a submarine . . ."
"It looks like a stopped gray heart . . ."
"The sky wears that color through which . . ."
"I always imagined that place . . ."
63 The New City

For my mother
and stepfather

I

FLYING

Sometimes late at night dozing over a book,
the fire low and the wind high outside,
I hear above the moan in the wires
the lonely motor of a small plane,
and I wonder who's up there or if,
through the overcast, he sees our lights
and can find his way safely down the blue runway.

I have been there once or twice hunched over red
instruments, intent on some horizon
at an unfelt altitude.
How slowly the night passed beneath my wings!
Yet the airspeed indicator read one hundred and two.
One of those lights down there was home,
small, indistinguishable in the darkness, and someone
pointing: "The star that moves—that's your father."

THE BARBER'S FOUNTAIN

The Italian barber
down our street
had a stone fountain
in his backyard.
When you turned it on
a small boy pissed.
And every day we listened
for someone to come
hissing with the news,
"He's turned it on,
come quick and see!"

After the barber died
his wife turned it off.
But one day
an orb weaver spun
a web from the penis
to the fountain rim.
And the barber's wife,
who feared spiders
worse than death,
turned it on again.

GRACE

You look away as though to pretend
you can't see the man aiming at us.
He must have stood for hours focusing,
shooting, holding out his card,
perhaps having already decided
who should pass and who stop.
Why are you dressed all in black?
You were never religious, no one has died.
You tow me past the theater, errant knight,
feet skipping off the pavement.

How famous we seem with that caption
above our heads, *Two Big Features!*
The Grapes of Wrath, Of Mice and Men.
After all these years I seem to see us
reversed: I the little angry mother
and you the son, unruly as always,
aiming a wooden sword
down the camera's muzzle, that breath
fixed and burning, that petrifying light.

DEPRESSION

He is pushing a black Ford
through an empty street—
a car like his father's
that beat the flat roads like wind
in summer and brought him here.

He never forgave his father.
That was the year he left home.
Then there was talk of weather
and everyone was packing.
Windmills were stopped
all over Kansas.

He is thinking of fathers,
the ways they never forgive you,
withholding love like lust.
But they quit, they stop like pumps.
There is no way to
set them working again.

He is thinking of mothers,
how she could not know how he
half followed girls down dark streets
of his heart, how that loneliness
is passed to sons,
to the fathers of sons.

He is pushing a black Ford.
Its problem is such a heart
you cannot give it enough care.
Like a father it will quit.
And there is no end to this.

MY FATHER

I have to remember you and I can't.
I call you shadow or sand.
No portrait or photo can keep you,
not even an old shirt or a shoe
that a dog might lie down by.
Still there is something,
this face that stares out of a cup,
a sound like a chair scraped back
in a room in which no one is sitting,
a thing like a stone or a root,
a bundle of rotting rags,
a whirlwind of dust and papers,
a name I hold now like a dead bird
from a country beyond affection or hate,
Prieto the dark one, the dishwasher.

HAVANA BLUES

Tonight I thought of you as I smoked a cigar
Smuggled in from your birthplace by a senator

Who gave it to a friend who gave it to me.
Why speak as though to someone I could see?

I try to know why fathers leave their sons.
Why it is easy to forget—it must be, when

You've never written me to say you're well—
If you're alive—and that you wish me well,

Would like to visit when you have a chance.
Were you too proud or grieved? The evidence

Suggests you were, and so I understand
And must forgive. If you would only send

A card to say Hello again! Your Father.
But I'm talking to myself. Why bother?

You might be dead for all I know or care.
I care, and yet I must confess my fear

Is finding you, not knowing what to say.
I'm talking to myself, a game I play

With words, your face the paper that I press,
Blank father, ghost! And if I miss

You now I miss for both of us. At two,
A small imperfect replica of you.

THE CAMERA

This eye does not become you,
though it contains you.
What you do not want to see
is, if only for that moment
when I press the shutter,
what you are, abstracted,
a bit cold.

Each year the circle of friends
grows smaller with you at stake.
Your friends suppose an intimacy,
not yours,
though one at least
must have wanted loyalty
beyond the personal.
Men change.
Not that much, you would add.
Like a photograph,
something is retained
which belongs to time
and pulls us apart.

The eye, like a shutter,
traps us in a pose
repeated for others.
So we are here?
No, we are caught in the brown study
of old photographs revisited
like the bad days of adolescence.
If change ruins friendships
I trust these damages to refine us.
I trust my friends to see beyond
self-interest,

as the eye of the camera records everything
but possesses no one.

Far down the film's unwinding
speculation of light,
two men, they could have been us,
the oldest explaining
as they descended
that broad winding stairway to the sea
the terms of combat,
the resolution of differences
a distant redeeming possibility.

That night,
the sea dark and strong,
the ship already down,
I woke thinking,
Yes, this is what it is like.
The friends are important,
but the heart, like a shutter,
must go alone,
opening, closing,
opening, closing.

EXPOSURES

For years I've tried
to capture you, my dear.
It should be easy
in the space we live in.
But the faces you wear!
Either I'm too close
or I haven't seen you.
In the first photograph
you wear a fox-fur hat.
Interesting the way
the light tips each hair.
The hat escaped with a thief.
The vicuña scarf you tried
for months to weave
into a poem is clear.
You can see each thread.
The face, though, is wrong.
By lamplight,
a dangerous half-moon.

In the second photo,
our daughter nearly six,
you seem more motherly,
a role you're seldom
comfortable in—who is?
Here the reproduction's
much too dark,
a Madonna-like benevolence

masks the ornery in you.
This time the camera lies.

Now, as you grow older,
I make you sexier
because you are,
a natural process
using light from leaves,
a half profile
under the cherry tree.
The telephoto tricks you,
my quick, unposeable bird.

The camera only sees
the lighter or the darker
side of you.
It may or may not see true.
Still the years show you
through the same lens
complimentary in any light,
if the eye that reads
exposure reads right,
and the hand that trips
the shutter doesn't shake.
As evidence I give
these yearly proofs of you.

THE BOOK OF THE DEER, THE BEAR AND THE ELK

You never wrote the small green book
like the poems of Edward Thomas.
It was a book I dreamed.
But watching the green report of your heart
on the monitor it came to me as I stood
like one of the doctors in my cap and gown,
home, where you've lived like a bachelor
at the far end of the house,
there is a green diary:
the book of the deer, the bear and the elk,
with snapshots of Julian and Bob and Harry,
old hunting friends
dead as the game strung up on poles
or drooped across fenders.

I think you are the only one left.
And still you fight to stay,
breathing the scorched air of the burn ward,
the sweet stink of your own charred flesh.
Stepfather, don't go.
Seventy-three years is not the end of the book,
the letters you never wrote,
because even before you blistered your hands
the act of writing pained you.

It took four shots to bring it down.
Your father never praised you.
Rising from dinner that night he beckoned
toward the woodshed where the skinned deer

hung draped in burlap.
Then he whipped you with a belt.
"Don't ever bring home meat
shot up like that!
One bullet is enough."
I saw you kill a running buck
at three hundred yards with one shot.
It's a brutal art that fathers pass to sons.

When the propane tank ignited
you took the flaming cylinder in your arms
like a lover
and fought it out the door.
Now you dream each night of the trailer burning.
My mother screams and beats the fire out of her hair.
She was not burned like you—
twice, and three times, for your care.

Now the deer are safe from us,
I have one photograph to add to our book:
a doe running through a field.
My best shot.
Somewhere in the grass behind her
a fawn is hiding.
You can't see it,
but it's there waiting for its mother
to draw us away.
Later, she'll return
and the two of them will be saved.
Stepfather, Father, be like the fawn.

II

RUNNING LIGHTS

Once we set the dead adrift
with a few provisions
they never came back.
But once we found the splinter
of a hull lodged between rocks
and said that was Sigurd's boat.

Now we embark hoping to return.
The simple offerings our wives make
blow away like smoke.
We know our families will flock for us
like birds on the beach
to count the crosses,
the red, green and white constellations
that one by one lift
out of the dark waves.

Once in a while one will be missing.
Perhaps we saw the flare in the night,
the falling star.
Thank God it did not fall for us.
Our fear of such events could not
last long: there were hulls to scrape,
nets that needed mending . . .

BUTCHERING CRABS

All day we smashed and swore,
filling the brine tanks
with twitching claws and legs,
white belly meat,
dropping the entrails
and deep-dish violet shells
down a slime hole to the bay.
Even Hawk, our best butcher,
got pinched.
Those claws cut
through our heaviest gloves.
When we broke them off
they clamped down tighter.

"Take that, you buckethead!"
the shell shattering
like crockery.
"You'll never bite another
Indian!"
Stabbing his hands
into that cage of maniacs,
clattering and seething,
bubbling at the mouths,
glare of stalked eyes,
claws like open traps,
he would snap one up
and in one smooth movement
break it over the knife.

She dips her fork
into the cocktail,
lifts it to her perfect face
and eats.
Over miles of white tablecloth
the bits and pieces fall.

He lived in a shack
with newspaper curtains,
drove home each night
crabby and skidding.
On the third day
they gave me my check:
"Too slow, sonny."
But Hawk was fast,
he was faster than life.

TAKE THE BASS FOR EXAMPLE

Take the bass for example.
Excellent fighter,
perfect parent,
it guards its nest,
the new young who circle it
like a constellation
around some giant
admirable star.
And then it strikes.
The young are scattered,
a few sacrificed
to that extreme hunger.
If we believe Nature is benign,
let us,
for the sake of the lesson
always the same,
say that it encourages survival
not of bass alone but
of the Idea of bass.

In the world of great ideas
such theories are cheap,
but generalize once too often
and you are struck
by your impertinence.
One must deal with particulars,
as the observant young bass,
seeing that huge smile
spreading beyond
the boundaries of good sense,
must begin to suspect,
despite prior evidence,
a new odd kind
of parental love.

FOR A FRIEND DROWNED OFF GRAYS HARBOR

Why must you reappear in the doorway
of the house fallen down behind you
through seasons of iron and lightning,
rain-corroded roofs?

In the harbor the fishing fleet creaks softly,
lifting, falling against its lines,
moored flocks of birds, odors of diesel and salt,
metallic stink of salmon.

Reeves, your face swims in the red glow of the binnacle,
reflecting in rain-streaked glass,
guiding me now under starlight
filtering through crossed bodies of birds.

The fish and fishing boat come to the same end:
ribs combing the sand, stripped masts and spars,
the engine that brought us safely in each night
an old iron chest seized by barnacles.

I found her compass swung in windows of a salvage yard,
saw salt water course down the glass in a blind fog,
seaward, heard tide-swung hammers of the entrance bell
tolling that no man might drown.

And I remember you standing in the hatchway
of the boat without running lights, as though
you had not foundered years ago in a storm one night,
just as you were turning the bow toward home.

GIANT OCEAN SUNFISH

First, I thought it was a man drowning,
but the hand that seemed too casual
became a flipper and then
a huge forehead with wings,
a giant spewed-up misshapen embryo,
its mouth little more than a beak.
I stared as it slipped past,
then left it glaring in my wake
like an old dull mirror.

Even though I knew what it was
it still makes no sense.
Old fishermen say
they drift that way for weeks,
as though dazed and helpless.
There is nothing you can do with them.
The natives call them *Mola Mola*
or headfish and occasionally eat them.
I try to imagine that huge morose meal.
At night, awash in the ocean's phosphorus,
they bask like moons,
separate and lonely.

SPIDER REEVES

But for the broken firing pin
would it have lived elsewhere?
You could have blown it out
with your breath, poked it out
with a stick, but you liked
to see its many eyes gleam
from the chamber
each time you opened it.
The next-door chamber took
in noisy tenants, threw them out.

What the spider thought
of that loud eviction?
It lived next door to death
no more a damned fool than you.
Smokeless powder, Damascus twist?
Lucky you didn't poach your own
head instead of the deer's.
One night you shot at eyes
and fetched a scream so shrill
you thought it was a woman's.

It was a ring-tailed coon's.
Who else but you would plug
a punctured gas tank with a match,
patch a leaking boat with gum,

get lost in fog on an ebb tide
with the wind building?

In school they called you Spider,
not for the spider in your gun,
but because you snagged passes
with your sticky hands
running so many directions at once
it seemed you had eight legs.

Now you run with the tide,
so many lost molecules,
a gleam in the dog shark's eye,
a diatomaceous spark.
You were not very bright.
You could have learned to live.

LISTENING TO BEETHOVEN ON THE OREGON COAST

About a quarter to ten the door softly opened
then closed again.
No one was there, no wind outside.
Earlier I'd watched two trawlers miles apart
work past the North Head lighthouse.
When I looked again they were gone.
Only the owl light of the beacon,
the distant whistle of a buoy,
and the surf wild from a storm miles out at sea.
Beyond the window, cliffs fall away in blackness.

There are wrecks out there,
sunken masts slanting up like crosses
on submerged churches,
bones of fishermen that flow away in phosphorus
past yellow eyes of lingcod,
flat ridiculous soles that walk the sea floor
like lost shoes.
Everything there broken, torn down, consumed.
Each tide a regurgitation of casualties
bleached by salt and moonlight.
Walking by night your feet kick sparks from sand,
the night cries of birds drown in the surf's roar.

III

INCOMPLETE DESCRIPTION OF "THE WORLD'S SMALLEST CHURCH GROTTO"

Past the NO PETS ALLOWED sign,
two bronze-colored plastic lions with turquoise eyes
guard the entrance,
and two green bullfrogs on orange lily pads,
a gray burro pulling an orange, yellow and white cart,
a ceramic mother duck with three baby rabbits,
the shell of a giant man-eating clam.

There are no paths but a series of meanders, most of which
avoid the charitable collection box and its pleading sign.
There is a raised cruciform flower bed
grouted with flower pots, plates, cups, jugs,
and Mrs. Butterworth syrup bottles.
Then a small stone windmill
sporting a foggy glass-domed clock,
always six forty-five,
a pair of Dutch wooden shoes
on a fluorescent-red plaque.
Each wind sail grows a forty-watt bulb.

Why ask what it means?
Only imagine, if you had had the vision of a saint
and were obsessed as a pack rat what you would do.
Walk past the two ponds to an abalone-shell wishing well,
its roof a thousand buttons, beads and mirrors;
and its neighbor phallus—
perhaps an earth god's, oddly pagan in this Christian place—
about six feet high and leaning,

of smoothly rounded, cemented-together stones.
In summer, a waterspout in its head
jets a rainbow over the grotto.

Suppose you have made your wish,
go then to the cryptlike display case
with two hand pumps atop
and crammed with crab shells, clam shells, cockle shells,
a pious choirboy singing *Gloria*
to a stuffed deer's head
mounted on a button-studded wooden shield
and wearing a lace collar,
antlers metallic gold,
nose Rudolphed with a red Christmas tree light,
above three Kiwanis Club Home Decorating Contest trophies.

Beyond the planter
with the sign DANGER DO NOT TOUCH THE CACTUS,
you'll find the place where the Virgin appeared,
to whom this continuing labor is devoted,
marked now with a small stone chapel.
Inside, a framed poem
"To Uncle John from his niece Jamie, age 10,"
and a portrait of the Savior
suffused with the inner light of an electric bulb,
but still managing a serene, straight face.

CLEAN SYMMETRICAL FURROWS

. . . sheer plod makes plow down sillion/Shine.
—Hopkins

If one plows the other ought to reap.
No. They both plow every other week.
It isn't harvesting, driving the Farmall
Round and round, or planting either.
Something keeps them on a tether
Like horses in a carnival
Pounding the sod down in a circle.

They take turns, pleasant old children,
Perfectly identical farmers in
Bibbed overalls and billed caps.
What does the mother think there on the porch,
Rocking and nodding, why doesn't she teach?
You can only show them so many steps.

Then they forget.

0°

Already he appears to disintegrate,
head wrenched in profile,
barely enough snow to cover
the juncture of wings, breast and head,
a shred of oak leaf stuck to his chest,
the skeleton's outline rising
through a pulp of orange and gray down,
and all around him spears
of dead grass, twigs and shredded leaves
aim through the snow.

His feet, maple twigs with curved shiny nails,
have simply let go.
He seems more fossil than recent casualty
failing into the landscape.
Or else the emblem of a defunct
European state
on the tattered background of a flag.

Only the powder-blue primaries
retain something of the speed
and curvature of flight,
as though flight's cunning alone
could hurl the whole mess,
skin, feathers and bones,
flaming into orbit and so oppose
this blind separation of powers.

DODO

Years they mistook me for you,
chanting your name in the streets,
pointing grubby fingers.
Today in the natural history museum
I saw why.
Dodo, you look the way I feel,
with your sad absentminded eyes
and your beak like a stone-age axe.
Even your feathers
dingy and fuzzy.
What woman would want them for a hat?

With a name like *Didus ineptus*
where could you go,
wings too small to fly with
and feet so large and slow?
You were not very palatable.
Men slaughtered you for sport.
Hogs ate the one egg you laid each year.
Sometimes I think I know how it feels
to be scattered over the world,
a foot in the British Museum,
a head in Copenhagen,
to be a lesson after the fact,
an entity in name only,
and that taken in vain.

THE BIRD MAN OF REDMOND

He will not be told
the rockcrusher's legal weight,
or why the courts consider
the rights of birds worth less
than gravel or money.
Therefore he may stand a few more days
with his arms spread in the clearing
crying "Here birds! Here birds!"
as the flocks gather for crumbs.

I have known others like him.
Filthy, kindly men, living alone,
friends to deer and chipmunk,
no longer able to speak sensibly
of the world outside,
though they babble to anyone who comes.
One, I heard, took to the trees
and was found years later,
his face chewed by rats.
Some swore him a genius
wronged in politics or love.

Sometimes I think there is in each of us
a simple place with its fire,
a place of refusals,
to forget whatever we came here for,
a face, no matter—
surely some awful failure.
Some call it the self
we must lure as slowly as the eyes
that come each night to circle the fire.
Most never find it.

I have dreamed such a place for years.
A room I had almost forgotten
in a house so huge it was hard to remember
each room and hallway.
I want so much to believe in it,
because I know that others have seen it too,
or some such place.

There are too many rockcrushers, too many
tempers that break every hardness but our own.
Just once I'd like some gentleness to win.
It may not.
Which is why we have these places in ourselves,
these rooms we barely remember.

THE CARDINAL

Not to conform to any other color
is the secret of being colorful.

He shocks us when he flies
like a red verb over the snow.

He sifts through the blue evenings
to his roost.

He is turning purple.
Soon he'll be black.

In the bar's dark I think of him.
There are no cardinals here.

Only a woman in a red dress.

SURGERY

Once it was a place for the watch to measure
the hours without disruption, to carry the ring.
It would hold a fork only to be polite.
The other, the hand that was quick and sure, is numb.
The surgeons whisper among themselves like fishermen
after dark, casting the sutures in, tugging them out.
Gradually the hand closes like the waters of a lake.
Tomorrow I will walk out wearing a new white claw
and set the slow hand to learning its letters.

"GO STUDY THE SPOTS ON A DAFFODIL"

You meant it as an insult, or I took it so.
It's true I've studied these things.
I don't want to write about racial insults,
the poverty of the poor, a poetry of larger
social consciousness, because I have been poor
and insulted, and it's a relief, after all,
in the time I have left, to look at flowers,
not to have to read the history of my life
written over and over by others as though
they themselves had lived it.

But for you, since you asked me to, I'll write
not what you imply I should, but what
I have always written out of love and necessity.
This poem is for you, Philip, with love.
The daffodils are not in bloom yet
and the first crocus has yet to show,
but yesterday I bought a beautiful fern.
In our living room it bursts and spills
like quiet green fireworks.

This morning I listened to some Bach partitas.
The pianist was happy, he hummed as he played,
tuneless, absorbed as I would like to be by this
fern, each note struck out of pain and pleasure,
repeating itself in the bright green atmosphere
as the fern is repeated outside our window
by camellia, rhododendron, maple and cedar—
names of things I like to repeat for their own
sakes, to investigate because you asked me to.

STALKING MORELS

We had hoped to find them beside the railroad tracks
or in deep shade beneath oaks, with mayflowers
and columbine, attending the jack-in-the-pulpit's
green sermon, shapes newly risen from sleep,
lewd, hollow-hearted sponges on stalks, half brain,
half cock, crumbs of earth clinging to their heads.
We had only their pictures to go by, instructions
on how they are always found in the same place,
persistent as old weather.
But everywhere we looked we found them wanting.

They were like ancestors dead before we were born,
whole nunneries withered away
in some inaccessible wilderness, their musk unsavored.
Now I am trying to let such forms lie as they may.
My mouth upon your neck denies their history,
a language I do not speak very well.
But if we could find them we could roll
like dogs in their bouquet,
wear their earthy-ethereal smell,
or nip them like hogs in passing,
seize their day in ours,
and never after regret their absence.

FLOOD CONTROL

No river should be allowed to do as it pleases.
Therefore this dam like two sides of a pyramid
closing the valley, the upper half flooded
and calm for miles under a white layer of ice,
the lower half turbulent.

We watched a father and child fly a kite
safely over the spillway, saw it dip and rise
then spiral down again in a light wind.
From where we stood we could feel the current
in that tunnel a hundred feet beneath us.

I cannot say what held us apart.
I suppose something like the dam,
a surface we could walk safely out on,
with the homelife in the valley sure beneath
thousands of acres of ice and a tower.

The river flows past our feet, mindless, pliable.
There was even something to be made of its fish,
their rolled rubber mouths spotting the surface
so that in late afternoon light a series of arrows
appeared to divide the sky's reflection,

our reflections, pointed not painted, as though
in compasses spinning at the North Pole.
For in summer our thoughts would turn to ice,
how pleasant that tinkling of ice in glass.
The drinks were like bells, a kind of enchantment.

Into what?
I see you as you were then
in your new summer dress, always conscious
exactly, of whatever effect you are making
and I wonder what you are contriving toward.

So many times I thought of writing or calling.
I imagined the floodgates opening on shining water
like a giant cash register on the right change.
Now I am struck by that vacancy:
objects releasing their strained significance,

remembering that the dam is a dam, the bridge
a bridge, and the river has its own way to go,
utilities not given to powers of reflection
but to flood control, access, the turning of turbines
in houses of power, the real power indifference.

As when we quit carping, and throw in the last bait
with no further attachments, the evening shimmers.
No need to cleanse our hands of success,
the lines put neatly away for another occasion,
and the fish, their scales like money, balancing.

IN THE MORE RECENT PAST

Difficult now to remember your face.
Sometimes another almost resembles,
but nothing, no one really . . .
The mind is such heavy earth
it bears us down
with worm riddles and faults.
In death, in the second
of absolute recall, I may find your image
cracked out of subterranean slate,
each detail preserved.
Then will I say, like God,
this was one of my failures?
Whatever I meant to accomplish
escapes me now, a chore of love,
I think, that found its opposite?
The shells we wore are empty.
They have turned to stone.
Somewhere in another death you may be
handling mine,
wondering how the creatures we were
escaped us.

THE BURNED GIRL

You will hold that face in mind
like a charred egg and find no relief
for this, no forgetting, no bird
to save you from memory of ashes
by climbing on burnt wings
through solutions of air.

You cannot march toward God
on this, the rainbow like a moon bridge
over the river of woes.
Look down now into the face
not even your own.
See how exactly it blisters and splits.
This way of suffering is impersonal and pure,
no occasion for raptures,
not yours to indulge in.

Her eyes, more than yours, will see
promise of beauty burned like a letter,
the graft of years knit scars
no scalpel or lightness of mind will excise.
Look down and find her there like poured lead
in the dark night of her days.

Hold that memory where islands keep
their blue distance,
where nothing is holy or firm.

THE DREAM OF EXECUTION

At dawn they led a man out and tied him to a stake.
They were going to shoot him and leave him there.
There was nothing anyone could do about it.
The commanding officer stood smoking a cigarette
while the firing squad composed mostly of conscripts
leaned nonchalantly on their rifles, and a priest
droned the last rites like a black fly in summer.
No one would come in the final moment with a pardon.
Whatever the man had done would be remembered—
possibly something as trivial as speaking out of turn.
The man looked around him as though unaware
that sentence had been passed, and he would die.

Just before the order was given they led a woman
into the courtyard, evidently for a last visit.
We heard her say to him in a high clear voice,
"If I love you, it is not for anything you have done."
And that was all; in a moment she was gone,
the man was dead, and the troops were marching away.
I don't know why I remember this sequence,
or why it keeps happening over and over as though
I were somewhere outside myself waiting for it to end,
to become something other than it is, her name
the one word opening like a bullet in his lung.

SMALL HUNTING ACCIDENT

Flat fields, a glare of ice swept free of snow.
Each step a hesitation and a falling through.
The hunter stumbling with each step wishes
that the ice would hold him, that the woman
who left yesterday would reclaim him.
He sees the fox prints, the bloodstained
snow-angel flurry of a killed pheasant, one feather.
As he stoops to pick it up his spine fails . . .

He thinks of what it is to die,
for the first time learns the loneliness,
the sorrow of lost animals,
remembers waking alone in the night dead,
though his heart beat wildly and his pulse raced.
A moment like the sudden flare
and glide of a flushed pheasant
he knew could not be there.
Struggling to rise the man thinks,
Is it just that what we take for granted escapes us?

Once the pheasant shone like jewelry.
Now there is only this feather.
Once that woman rose from my bed and combed her hair.
Now she is gone, her letters are chitchat.
Words are pheasants and then they are foxes.

A plane departs, and when it lands
the passengers are changed.
A man kneels in the snow to study death
and remembers a woman, a mouth he had kissed,
its small white scar like vapor in the blue.

When a shock from a life gone wrong
sends its impulse to the right nerve
and brings a proud man to his knees
what does he do?
He unloads his gun to use as a crutch.
He ties branches to his feet.
He says to the woman as though she were there,
"Come spring my thoughts will leave you like the snow.
There will be no hatred between us.
The blankness of this space, the pain I feel
with each step will inspire something,
as a silence among friends provokes talk,
yes, even of weather."

ONE BOOK

Toward the last
he preserved one
clean well-lighted
room and one book
to be opened when
there was nothing
to do but read
whatever he had
not thought
to write down.

On a small table
the book lay waiting
its pages uncut
a knife beside it.

He entered the room
picked up the knife
and began to read
full of regret
for the undone
the undoing.

THE FOUR SEASONS

*

In the shape of a submarine
frost lengthens on a window.
Outside, winter sparrows perch
in rhinoceros-colored trees.
Mare's tails chase whitely
past brick chimneys.
I have seen those lights before,
small rectangular eyes
of far buildings, one church
steeple darkening the blue sky.

*

It looks like a stopped gray heart,
if hearts sport such delicate scallops
and trees wear hearts on their sleeves.
Now the first wasp of spring emerges,
its wings a transparency of fish scales,
old isinglass or vein-fretted windows—
wings of the first untranscendent angel
sentenced to death by the god frost.
How can some later spring reclaim this
paper city or repair its walls damaged
in the long drop from the one hundred
and twentieth odd year of a tree?

*

The sky wears that color through which
you expect a tornado's black drill.
Only cicadas try the air, a scratching
that cannon could not silence.
Beyond the barn with three siloes
and the wind pump stopped like a tin daisy,
carp lip the surface of reflected sky,
the promised violence.

*

I always imagined that place
as an orchard on a mountaintop,
its summer Delicious freckling
to a sunset by Seurat.
But the last time it was fall,
the sere grass bent one way
toward an open gate,
as though a great wind had swept
down stones of the garden walls.
Two posts bent where the orchard
had been, their purpose obscure.
They stood, I think, where flowers
had rivaled deepest
in their colors and scents.

THE NEW CITY

Everything will be old,
even the odors drafting
from the river,
clearer or muddier
than the rivers at home.
Home will be the place
never entirely left,
as you see after long miles
through flat country,
the outpost organized into
checkerboards of light
and recall an advantage
lost once
in a last sudden move.

For now, the river spreads
its unfamiliar patterns
of light, trees and anti-trees,
buildings carved
by a passing duck,
wavery as in an earthquake,
then still,
or barely trembling
in the aftershock
of subsurface disturbance,
salvoed by a fish
and again re-healed,
as though it mirrored more
than its own place,
that other indestructible city

still reverberating rings or years,
a fish's gold leap,
the entire life of a tree.
Why should bleak chimneys
and stained brick walls,
as I saw them once in winter
just before the river froze,
why should these awake such pangs,
when mountains and water
rise and fall around me
with so little disturbance?

There was something I left
I always come back to.
It has the feeling of place,
as the river,
if it remembered,
could recall the flight down
as rain
into the shimmering anonymity
of a new life,
the summit before the great fall
and rush to the sea,
the reflective passage
beneath factories and bridges,
slower and slower,
as if reluctant to return always,
however changed in outward appearance,
to the same place.

It makes no difference
that both rivers flow
into a sea

and that the seas connect,
so you can say without mysticism
it all comes to one
or, as you would put it,
it makes no difference.
Say I passed here once as part
of the seasonal transient debris
and left no mark,
but that I wrote the date down,
thinking to write more at leisure.
In 1912 the water reached this high,
and I, somewhat lower,
would have perished if I'd stayed,
unborn as a tulip in February
washed out of its bed.
Human, to picture events
before one's conception,
to remember the past
as it never was,
the city perfectly distorted
by imperfect memory:
Gary become Venice or Paris.

So it is possible to stand upon
this shore littered with tires,
bedsprings, bottles and cans,
and feel something like clear water
rising until it brims and spills,
and the truth of that other place
is washed into a beautiful calm.
Even here, by the river,

a great sea crashes
and ebbs around me,
large bright-colored fish
turn, barely visible
beneath its surface.
Once I would have caught them,
watched without remorse
as their colors paled
and grew dull.
Now it is enough
to know they are there,
and that the city,
the other city
with its old gray walls,
shines over the water.

Henry Carlile was born in San Francisco and grew up in the Pacific Northwest. He attended the University of Washington and, since 1967, has taught at Portland State University. During 1978-80 he was a visiting lecturer in the Iowa Writers' Workshop. His first book, *The Rough-Hewn Table*, won a Devins Award in 1971. He lives in Portland, Oregon, with his wife, Sandra McPherson, and daughter Phoebe.